BRITAIN IN OLD PHOTOGRAPHS

PRESTON

A L A N   G .   C R O S B Y

Budding
BOOKS

A Budding Book

First published in 1995 by Alan Sutton Publishing Limited

This edition published in 2000 by Budding Books, an imprint of Sutton Publishing Limited
Thrupp · Stroud · Gloucestershire GL5 2BU

Copyright © Alan G. Crosby, 1995

A catalogue record for this book is available from the British Library

ISBN 1-84015-183-8

This book has been printed exclusively for: Book Clearance Centre, 6 Marketwalk Shopping Centre,
Chorley, Lancashire PR7 1DE

Typesetting and origination by
Sutton Publishing Limited.
Printed and bound in England by
J.H. Haynes & Co. Ltd, Sparkford.

Compiled from the collections of the Harris Museum & Art Gallery by Dr Alan Crosby

One of the earliest and most impressive of Preston mills was the aptly nicknamed Big Factory, built by Swainson & Birley in Fishwick in 1835. The contrast between the old agricultural world, where cows graze peacefully, and the mushrooming industrial might of Preston is eloquently conveyed in this 1840s view.

Contents

Fortunately for later generations the photographers of Preston from the 1850s to the 1950s were not content to record only the grand, the dignified and the respectable faces of the town and its life. In the early years of the twentieth century many scenes of slums and back streets, industries and poverty were photographed. Here, in Mount Pleasant off Heatley Street, are handloom weavers' cottages built in the 1790s; the boarded-up windows of the cellar dwellings can be seen clearly.

Introduction

'Proud Preston', as the town has been known for centuries, has a fascinating and varied history. It began as a country market town, serving the Fylde and mid-Lancashire as well as the passing trade on the main north–south road, and continues to be a shopping centre of major significance – it is claimed to be the third most important centre in the north-west after Manchester and Liverpool. From an early date, too, Preston was an administrative centre because of its geographical position at the very heart of the historic county of Lancashire. 'Time-honoured Lancaster' may claim to be the county town – an issue which has generated much controversy in the columns of the local press during the mid-1990s – but for three hundred years Preston has been the place from which the county has been governed, the real centre of power within Lancashire.

In the seventeenth and eighteenth centuries Preston was an important centre for the gentry and nobility, many of whom lived near the town, and for part of the year it was the focus of their social life. The Preston 'season' was the Lancashire equivalent of the seasons of places such as Tunbridge Wells and Bath, with horseracing and cockfighting, dances and assemblies. The town was, according to Defoe in the early eighteenth century, a place of lawyers and merchants – and that legacy is still apparent, in the architectural charms of Winckley Square and the attractive walks around the edge of Avenham Park as well as in the numerous legal and financial concerns listed in Yellow Pages and announced by discreet brass plaques on converted Georgian and Victorian houses.

Preston was a river port from early times, although because of its position 18 miles up a muddy estuary it could never compete with Lancaster and Liverpool. However, in 1885 the magnificent and daring venture of building a vast new dock was undertaken, and for a few decades Preston's role as a port was transformed. The river was perpetually dredged to provide the deep water access which was essential, and the dock estate developed a range of warehousing and storage concerns, but the costs were very high. In the long-term, high costs, inadequate access and changing patterns of shipping and commerce put an end to the hopes of the Victorians, and the port was closed. Its legacy today is a great expanse of water which has become a major local recreational attraction.

Above all perhaps, in the nineteenth and early twentieth centuries Preston was a cotton town. This was never to the exclusion of its other roles, but for a hundred years cotton was the largest single element in the town's economy. It altered the face of Preston for ever. The country market town became a great industrial centre, the skyline a forest of chimneys, and the fields around were swamped beneath a flood of terraced housing. The new middle classes, the cotton managers and the administrators, built more genteel suburbs, such as

Fulwood and Ashton, and the town expanded to absorb its neighbouring rural communities. There were other industries, like cotton, with the legendary name of Horrocks, and some – notably Dick Kerr and its tramcars – which carried the name of Preston around the world. But now most of the old industries have gone. The 1950s and '60s saw the end of cotton as a major component of the town's economic base, while the slump of the early 1990s saw the closure of British Aerospace and Thorn Lighting.

Of course, Preston still has many industries, reflected in the Trades Procession held during the famous Guild every twenty years, but none is large enough to dominate in the way that cotton once did, and none is synonymous with the name of the town. Instead, Preston has once more become primarily a commercial and service centre, a reversion to the position of three hundred years ago. Shops and retailing, lawyers and accountants, merchants and traders, professionals and small businesses – the same elements which made up the town's economy in the late seventeenth century – have regained their pre-eminence. But all the many and diverse roles which the town has experienced over the past four hundred years have left their mark upon its character and appearance, and looking at Preston today we see a complex historical jigsaw puzzle. Sometimes only faint traces of the past remain, perhaps detectable only to those with knowledge of local history, while other features are more obviously 'historic'.

To find out more about the town's past we can investigate a wide range of sources. There are several published histories, ranging from that written by Richard Kuerden in 1682 and published in 1818, to the most recent, David Hunt's fine *History of Preston* which appeared in 1992. There is an abundance of documentary evidence, including the records of town and county, now in the Lancashire Record Office, and the papers of individuals, firms, societies and estates which are the raw material for so much historical investigation. There is also, crucially, the evidence of pictures, engravings, drawings and photographs – in no other way can we obtain a real impression of how the town looked and felt during the past 150 years. In this compilation the large collection of photographs which has been accumulated by the Harris Museum since the early years of this century has been used to present a survey of Preston between the 1860s and the 1940s.

From the early 1860s the town was fortunate to have several outstanding photographers, who left for posterity a superb legacy of high-quality images. These photographers – to the delight of later historians – were not content to stay in their studios. They went out and about, recording street scenes and industrial life, architectural splendours and the fast-vanishing legacy of ancient buildings and lanes. Many of these splendid pictures are reproduced here, together with the work of their successors up to the Second World War. Here are shown the elegant residences of the wealthy lawyers and cotton merchants, the tightly packed slums where the workers lived, the beautiful sailing vessels in the dock and the electric trams of the Edwardian era. Some scenes will be familiar, but many have long since vanished and will evoke powerful nostalgia among those who knew Preston before the 1930s. Parts of the town have changed beyond recognition, and most of its traditional industries have now vanished, but in this collection of photographs the old Preston is recaptured.

PROUD PRESTON:
CIVIC AND PUBLIC LIFE

*The magnificent Victorian town hall, built in
1862–7 to the designs of Sir George Gilbert Scott,
was a familiar landmark to generations of Preston
people. The building, a triumph of architecture and
inventiveness (the space which it occupied was
surprisingly small) replaced a Georgian building of
1762. The Victorian town hall, with its lavish
interiors and elaborate and impressive exterior, was
crucial to the fine visual quality of the town centre.*

On the night of 14/15 March 1947 the splendid town hall was gutted by fire, an event which is still sincerely lamented by many Prestonians. This dramatic photograph, taken when the blaze was at its height, emphasizes the scale of the disaster which befell the town on that fateful night.

On 15 March 1947, the morning after the disastrous fire, charred and fallen timbers, twisted metalwork, and cracked flaking stone are all that is left of the once-fine building. Despite many calls for full restoration the truncated remnant of the town hall was eventually demolished in 1962, and on the site rose Crystal House, an office block typical of its time and one which, in marked contrast to its predecessor, has failed to gain any popularity with the people of Preston.

The town was elaborately decorated in 1885 when the Prince of Wales (the future Edward VII) came to perform the official ceremony to start building work on the new dock. Here is the huge and somewhat incongruous 'medieval' archway which spanned the Fishergate railway bridge.

The mayor, Councillor Hunt, greets the less-than-cheerful Prince of Wales (later Edward VIII) on his arrival at Preston railway station during a tour of the depressed areas of north-west England in June 1927.

In 1938, the year after their coronation, King George VI and Queen Elizabeth toured Lancashire, paying brief visits to a lengthy list of boroughs. Here, on 17 May, they are seen arriving at Preston town hall for a civic reception. The king looks scarcely any happier than his brother had done eleven years before.

The official unveiling ceremony of the cenotaph in 1925, commemorating the 2,000 men of Preston who died in the First World War. The whiteness of the new monument contrasts sharply with the sooty blackness of the surrounding buildings.

Some of the workers of Gregson & Monks. During the Second World War many Preston factories produced armaments and other goods for the war effort. Gregson & Monks, loom manufacturers, switched to the production of shells.

In August 1945 victory was celebrated throughout the country by civic services and parades. Here in Preston military and civilian personnel march past huge crowds along Fishergate and past the town hall.

W.P. Sherwood's dramatic painting of crowds outside the Bull and Royal during the 1862 by-election. In the election, caused by the resignation of Richard Assheton Cross of Red Scar (one of the two Conservative members), Sir Thomas Hesketh (Conservative) defeated George Melly of Liverpool (Liberal) by 1,527 votes to 1,014.

The Preston branch committee of the Independent Labour Party, meeting at their rooms in Glovers Court beneath a bust of Lenin and portraits of Stalin and Keir Hardie, 1924. The thin man in the centre is Percy Taylor, the prosperous Preston cotton merchant who was the father of the famous historian A.J.P. Taylor.

The Corn Exchange and Public Hall was a fondly remembered Preston landmark. This 1901 view shows the glazed arcade and *porte-cochère*. The rear of the building was demolished in the late 1980s for the new Ringway extension, but the front – the oldest part – has been restored and survives as the Corn Exchange public house.

The original Corn Exchange was built in 1824; its elegant front block, topped by a small clock tower, gave access to a rear extension which served as a market hall. In the mid-nineteenth century this extension was often the scene of public events such as balls and banquets, and by the 1870s this had become its main purpose. This remarkable photograph shows the dinner given by the Wesleyan Methodists for 1,932 scholars, teachers and assistants in the rear market hall of the Corn Exchange on 29 May 1856, to celebrate the peace at the conclusion of the Crimean War. The diners consumed 2,000 lb of potatoes, 360 lb of bread, 900 lb of beef and about 700 lb of plum pudding.

In 1882 the Corn Exchange was extended, upgraded, and rechristened the Public Hall. This view shows a meeting of the Preston masonic lodge in the Public Hall in 1908. The high quality of the interior, with its fine organ and attractive arches and capitals with accompanying wrought-iron work, is very clear.

The old town hall and guildhall, painted by J. Ferguson in the mid-1850s. The attractive red-brick buildings were constructed in 1760, ready for the 1762 Guild, after their medieval predecessors began to fall down. They lasted only a century, being replaced in 1862 by the ill-fated Victorian town hall.

A treadmill was installed in the House of Correction, at the end of Church Street, in 1825. It was used to draw water from wells and to grind corn. This posed photograph shows the replacement wheel of 1891, which accommodated sixty-one prisoners. The wheel was abandoned in 1903, as a result of changing government policies.

In 1866 land at Deepdale was used for the new hospital (seen here in about 1900), which in 1897 received the patronage of Queen Victoria under the official title of the Preston and County of Lancaster Royal Infirmary. Much extended and expanded, the PRI treated thousands of Prestonians until its final closure in 1986.

During the First World War a temporary military hospital for the convalescence of wounded servicemen was erected on Moor Park. This view shows some of the prefabricated buildings, in use between 1915 and 1919.

This beautiful photograph of The Willows, Ashton, was taken in 1863. The dusty track has now been transformed unrecognizably, into the dual carriageway Riversway, but in 1863 it was a very quiet country lane which led out of the town and along the edge of the Ribble marshes. In the four-wheeled carriage are Doctors Hall and Noble, perhaps doing their rounds?

Mrs Abley, a Preston postwoman, photographed on 9 December 1916. During the First World War women were employed in many occupations from which they had hitherto been excluded.

Members of the volunteer fire brigade, photographed in about 1896 outside the Tithebarn Street fire station which was built in 1852. A steam engine was acquired in 1872 but the men were all volunteers: in 1883 they were paid 2s 6d for the first hour of each fire, 1s 6d per hour thereafter, and 9d per hour while they were watching on the premises.

Section Two

THE PRESTON GUILD

WEAVERS Comp^Y

The celebrated Guild is one of the most important elements in Preston's strong sense of civic identity. Here, in the 1802 Trades Procession, members of the newly powerful weavers company carry a working handloom which is operated by a small boy.

During the 1862 Guild the weather was exceptionally bad. This engraving shows the annual show of the Royal North Lancashire Agricultural Society at Penwortham Holme. The event was a wash-out – the river rose, flooded the site, and carried away the temporary wooden access bridge seen on the left.

At the 1862 Guild the foundation stone of the new town hall was laid by the Guild Mayor, Robert Townley Parker of Cuerden, in the presence of a huge crowd of spectators.

The Trades Procession grew in scale and splendour in successive nineteenth-century Guilds. This view of London Road from the 1862 Guild shows (right) the fishermen's float, complete with boat and oilskins, and on the left the borough fire brigade.

A superb photograph of the triumphal arch which was erected across Fishergate for the 1862 Guild. On the left is the distinctive Byzantine-style tower of the Fishergate Baptist Church, opened in 1858. The open aspect of the 'country' end of Fishergate is striking, with the gardens of large late eighteenth-century houses still fronting the road. The posters are advertising special Guild attractions, including opera at the Theatre Royal which was just beyond the arch.

The Guild Mayor's Procession on the opening day of the 1902 Guild: the Guild Mayor, Lord Derby, can be seen near the head of the procession, with his chaplain and the recorder of the borough.

For the 1902 Guild street decorations were elaborate and patriotic, with many Union flags in evidence. This is the Fishergate triumphal arch; the slogan 'Stanley for Ever' is a tribute to Lord Derby, the Guild Mayor. On the left is the Theatre Royal, advertising Gilbert and Sullivan's *Yeomen of the Guard*.

A formal portrait of Frederick, sixteenth Earl of Derby. Lord Derby was the Guild Mayor in 1902; he is shown wearing the ornate chain of office and fur-trimmed robes, and seated on the mayoral chair in the town hall.

At the opening of the first day of the Guild Court in 1902, Lord Derby is seated in the centre, with the clerk of the Guild at the table below him. Around them are the members of the Corporation, leading local dignitaries, and the Corporation officers bearing the maces and other items of the regalia.

The market place decorated for the 1902 Guild. Market Street itself had recently been completed and the new block of shops and offices on its south side is prominent in the photograph.

During Guilds photographers recorded not only the grand formal occasions but also the casual moments before and after Guild week. Here, in Fishergate, passers-by are captured for posterity just before the Guild of 1902: note the shawl and clogs of the woman crossing the road.

The Miller Arcade was decked in flags, bunting and swags of cloth for the 1922 Guild.

Looking not unlike extras from Gilbert and Sullivan, the officers of the Corporation are seen here in 1902 posing in their impressive robes and carrying the borough regalia which form such an important symbolic element in every Guild.

The formal prelude to Guild Week is the series of three public proclamations of the forthcoming celebration and of the legal renewal of burgess-ship which is at its heart. Proclamations have been made by each Guild Mayor since at least the fourteenth century. In August 1922 the Guild Mayor, Henry Astley-Bell, is seen making the third and final proclamation from the steps of the town hall.

From the late eighteenth century onwards individual firms and different trades vied with each other at every Guild to produce ever more ingenious and novel ways of advertising their wares and displaying their work. Here, from the 1922 Guild, is the cart representing Margerisons, the Preston soap makers. It carried a gigantic hand-carved block of soap weighing 6 tons.

The 1922 Guild was the last in which the cotton industry was dominant. Thereafter its collapse was swift and traumatic, and at the 1952 Guild it had a much diminished role. In 1922 the might of cotton was symbolized by a triumphal arch across Stanley Street built almost entirely of bales of cotton.

Schoolchildren participated in every Guild from 1842. Pageants became a standard feature, involving a great deal of excitement and a lot of time spent in rehearsal. The 1922 pageant, probably the most ambitious in any Guild, portrayed the town's history. Here the 'medieval guildsmen' gather for feasting and drinking.

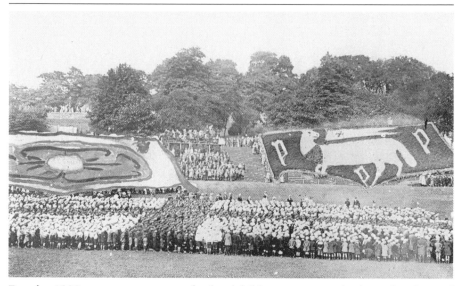

For the 1922 pageant an army of schoolchildren was organized on the slope of Avenham Park to display the red rose of Lancashire and the lamb and flag emblem of Preston, each child holding up a piece of coloured cloth to create the vast images.

The beautifully dressed girls of the Ribbleton Avenue Methodist Sunday School, getting ready to walk in the Nonconformist Churches Procession at the 1922 Guild.

Section Three

AN INDUSTRIAL
TOWN

*John Horrocks's Yellow Factory or Yard Works, between Church Street and Dale Street,
was built in 1791. It was the first large cotton mill in the town, and marked the
foundation of a great cotton empire which was intimately associated with Preston and its
people in the nineteenth century.*

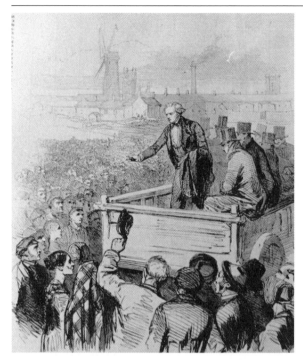

In the mid-nineteenth century Preston experienced a succession of traumatic events, beginning with the cotton depression and shooting of five strikers in Lune Street in 1842. In 1853–4 the Great Lockout, when workers demanding pay increases were locked out of the mills by the masters, became internationally famed – Marx thought that revolution might begin here and said that 'our St Petersburg is at Preston'. George Cowell, leader of the operatives, is seen addressing workers in Chadwick's Orchard.

Seven years after the capitulation of the workers in the Great Lockout the cotton industry was again brought to its knees, this time by the Cotton Famine during the American Civil War. Distress was acute in all cotton towns – in Preston between one-quarter and one-third of the population was officially classed as destitute, and soup kitchens such as these were a lifeline for the town's starving families.

In the spring of 1862, as the Cotton Famine wrought havoc in the town's main industry, thousands of people were put out of work. Local gentlemen and the Corporation proposed schemes for public works to relieve unemployment, including the landscaping of Moor Park. This photograph shows the ceremony of 'turning the first sod' in the summer of 1862.

The confusion of poor housing, mills, chimneys and railway cuttings which characterized the parts of Preston just outside the old town is exemplified in this view of Wellfield Road (middle distance) and the surrounding area, taken from the tower of St Mark's Church in about 1890.

John Horrocks died in 1804 but the business which he founded prospered in the next half-century. Several more mills were built, and the successor of the original firm, Horrockses Crewdson & Co., eventually occupied an extensive site at the end of Church Street. The imposing office building and gateway on London Road were built in 1912.

Centenary Mill in New Hall Lane, dating from 1895, was one of the last mills to be built in Preston. These red-brick giants with steel frames were much lighter and airier than their predecessors: the huge windows are well shown in this 1912 view.

The popular image of a cotton town is exemplified by this view of Greenbank Mill, Plungington, in the mid-1920s. The imposing buildings of the mill itself (founded in 1836) tower above the regular streets of closely packed terraced housing.

Views of mill interiors rarely show work in progress – it was too difficult to photograph the frenzied activity. Instead, photographers came for special occasions, when the mill was decorated and the workforce was allowed a break from operations. At the Yard Works in Stanley Street in 1918, weavers at Horrockses pause for the camera – second left is Nellie Brown and fourth left her sister Annie.

Workers in an unidentified Preston weaving shed celebrate the coming of age of the owner's son, *c*. 1910.

In 1918 peace, after four harrowing and heartbreaking years of war, was celebrated with enthusiasm at most mills. The typical decorations of paper chains and streamers are shown here, as the workforce assemble for the photographer at the great Tulketh Mill.

At Tennyson Road weaving shed there were no decorations in evidence, but a photograph was still taken – a very moving visual record of the workers who were the backbone of Preston's greatest industry.

Mill interiors were very dramatic, as this photograph of the vast cardroom at the Centenary Mill in 1920 demonstrates. In the cardroom the cotton fibres were drawn out, stretched, and then twisted to be wound round the bobbins, which formed serried ranks, row upon row.

The weaving shed at Fishwick Mills, 1920: this mill specialized in 'fine zephyrs, shirtings, voiles, poplins and other fancy goods'. Again, the scale and dramatic visual effect of the great weaving sheds is apparent.

In the older mills conditions were cramped and the lighting was often poor, as this photograph – taken in the winding room at Aqueduct Street mill in 1906 – suggests.

Simpsons' Gold Thread Works, in Avenham Lane, was one of Preston's more unusual industries, making very fine and delicate wires from precious metals. It was founded in 1822 and closed in the mid-1980s. In this view Stephen Simpson is seen with his family at their home, East Cliff House. Back row, left to right: Helen, Mary, Stephen senior, -?-, Stephen junior. Second row: Caroline, Isaac, Jane, Florence. Front row (seated on floor): Nona, Beatrice.

Robert Preston, a Simpsons' employee, at the Gold Thread Works on his 68th birthday in 1913.

In the 1850s the North of England Railway Carriage & Iron Company came to Strand Road, and in the 1870s new buildings were constructed. In this photograph, taken in about 1885, the undeveloped dock estate is in the foreground. Behind are St Walburge's spire and the chimneys of Wellfield Mill; in the centre are St Mark's Church tower with the prominent houses of Wellington Terrace; and West View Terrace and the chimneys of Aqueduct Street mills are to the left. The 1994 demolition of British Aerospace, as the site eventually became, has once more opened up this view.

Preston's own tramway network was comparatively small, but during the late nineteenth and early twentieth centuries the great Dick Kerr works built tramcars for the world. Here new trams are seen in the yard in about 1900. Those in the foreground were destined for Carlisle, the others for Sheffield.

An interior shot of the Dick Kerr works, showing the shells of tramcars under construction.

A view of Strand Road, *c.* 1898, showing the United Electric Car Co. works on the right. The clock on the elegant tower shows two minutes past twelve: the crowds in the street are just emerging from the works for their dinner break. It would not be wise to stroll in Strand Road today!

The Strand Road works, a major industrial complex with its own iron-moulding foundries, *c.* 1925. On the extreme right is Harry Bryan (1904–68), and third from the right is Jack Butler.

Preston was an important engineering centre. Here a trade photograph shows the huge flywheels built by Joseph Foster and Co. in 1930 for the winding engines on the cable-worked São Paulo railway incline in Brazil.

Cockshaw's Brushworks, at the corner of Market Street and Great Shaw Street, was an older craft industry. The works, photographed in 1920, produced hand-made brushes of exceptional quality. For the Preston Guild Cockshaw's produced special commemorative brush sets: some of these are now in the Harris Museum.

One of the most remarkable survivors of Preston's industrial past is the windmill at Cragg's Row, off Moor Lane. In the early nineteenth century the town had numerous windmills, but most of them had gone by the 1870s, demolished and replaced by steam power. This mill not only survived these changes but has remained to the present day, an unexpected sight among the tower blocks and office buildings.

The district around New Hall Lane had small brickpits for centuries, but most of them disappeared during the mid-nineteenth century as the town grew. In the vicinity of Waverley Road a brickworks lasted long enough to be photographed in 1885: the bricks were hand-thrown, and in this posed view the different stages in the making of bricks are displayed – from the raw clay on the right to the stacks of fired bricks on the left.

Preston Corporation built an electric power station just outside the borough, on the left bank of the Ribble at Penwortham, in 1923–4. In 1942 work began on a second power station, and this is shown in 1944, as yet uncompleted and with its chimneys painted in camouflage for protection against enemy aircraft.

Section Four

THE RIVER AND
THE DOCK

The Ribble from Whinfield House, Ashton, c. 1862. Until the dock was built the river flowed closer to
Ashton, near the line of the modern dual carriageway. It was edged by flat marshland, and the houses
on the hillside had an uninterrupted view of the vessels which came up to the quayside at the foot of
Fishergate Hill. Whinfield House was built for Henry Newsham Pedder, and was later occupied by
Edmund Harris, Preston's greatest benefactor.

This view, looking upstream from Whinfield House in 1863, is one of the few early photographs to show the site of the later dock. On the right is Penwortham Marsh; the rutted track in the foreground has become a trunk road, and the face of the valley has been transformed for ever by the building of the dock in the 1880s and by the recent redevelopment of the dock estate.

The first bridge at Penwortham was built in 1753 but fell down three years later. Its replacement, one of the best eighteenth-century bridges in Lancashire, is seen here in 1862 before the setting was disfigured by the adjacent railway bridge. In the foreground is the ancient foot ferry which linked the boathouse at Middleforth with the far end of Broadgate – by the 1860s this was an 'occasional' ferry, used only for leisure.

Broadgate was laid out from the early 1840s with middle-class housing along the river, and more tightly packed terraces inland. Its attractive character has survived, and some of the houses are now listed as being of special architectural and historical interest. The riverbank, seen here in the mid-1920s, was altered by the building of defence walls after the severe floods of 1927.

For centuries there were no bridges across the Ribble between Walton le Dale and Ribchester, but in the 1820s a new crossing was provided on the turnpike road at the foot of Brockholes Brow, close to the present Tickled Trout hotel. Because of the toll for foot passengers it was immediately christened 'The Halfpenny Bridge'. The building of the M6 in the 1950s means that the tranquil rural scene is now virtually unrecognizable.

The Ribble is a 'proper' river, not tamed or canalized, and it rushes extravagantly over its rocky bed. It can still produce some impressive floods, but in the past flooding was much more severe; in this 1936 view looking upstream from London Road bridge the whole valley has become a great lake, and Fishwick Bottoms are entirely underwater.

The river can also freeze – even now it is not uncommon for ice floes to come up on the tide, and for the channel to be more or less frozen over at the foot of Fishergate Hill. This marvellously atmospheric shot was taken from that location during the bitter frosts of February 1895, when the Ribble froze solid from shore to shore.

The river below Penwortham New Bridge (built in 1915) has retained a little of its old character even today. In this undated view, probably taken in the 1920s, the smoking chimneys of the Strand Road factories share the skyline with St Mark's and St Walburge's Churches, while small boats are moored along the bank as their successors are to this day.

The Danish schooner *Dagny*, beached in the channel of the Ribble at low water, 1919. In the background can be seen the arch of the new Penwortham bridge, with (behind the bridge) the roof of St Stephen's Church, which was demolished in March 1995.

On 17 July 1885 the Prince of Wales (later Edward VII) came to Preston to lay the foundation stone of the dock which was to bear his name – Albert Edward. Here he performs the ceremony in the presence of the mayor, the Corporation, other local dignitaries and a huge crowd of onlookers.

Building the great new dock involved diverting the Ribble into a new half-mile long channel to the south of the site. This rare view, taken in 1885, shows the excavation of the diversionary channel well under way.

Work on the immense project took seven long and expensive years, and not until 25 June 1892 was the dock ready for the official opening, performed by Prince Alfred, Duke of Edinburgh. In this photograph part of the royal procession is seen heading down Fishergate.

Timber, much of it from the Baltic and South America, was one of the most important commodities handled by Preston dock. The huge stacks of wood ranged along the dockside were a familiar site, but despite its bulk and importance almost all of the timber was unloaded manually. This photograph is undated, but was taken probably in about 1900.

An impressive array of vessels, both steam and sail, at Preston dock, *c.* 1920. In the distance is the Preston skyline, with St Mark's tower and St Walburge's spire, prominent landmarks as they are today, when almost all the shipping has gone and the recently landscaped dock is a favourite place for Sunday afternoon walks.

'Dumb hopper barge no. 3' is in the foreground in this view taken in the early years of the twentieth century. The barge, built in 1886 and broken up in 1952, was one of a fleet which performed an essential task – in conjunction with the port's dredgers they worked continuously to keep open the 18 miles of river between the dock and the Irish Sea.

The *Fresno City*, 1929. This general cargo vessel was the first ship to bring pine to Preston from Colombia, beginning a trade which later became of major importance to the dock.

An aerial view of the dock estate, 1923. On the left is the new river channel and the first Penwortham power station under construction. The network of railway sidings serving the dock is very clear, as are the almost undeveloped open fields to the north, where Blackpool Road and its housing estates would soon be built.

'White mice' unloading china clay at Preston Dock, *c.* 1910. The clay was used for finishing in the paper industry. Large quantities were imported to Preston from Cornwall, and the dust got everywhere – hence the nickname. A worker recalled: 'The grab brought the clay out and into a hopper where it went into these little bogeys . . . on railway lines.'

Section Five

TRANSPORT

*The Tram Bridge, 1862. This remarkable photograph shows the original (and by that time
very decrepit) bridge carrying the horse-drawn tramway which linked the northern and
southern halves of the Lancaster Canal. The tramway included a chain-worked incline at
Avenham, and this can be seen in the background. At the northern end of the bridge is the
wooden structure housing the winding drum for the chain. The tramway, which was opened
in 1805, finally closed in 1863 but the bridge was well used by pedestrians and so
survived – although subsequently rebuilt in concrete.*

The northern section of the Lancaster Canal is now very busy with pleasure craft, and ever since the early nineteenth century it has been popular for leisure use. This photograph of the old Woodplumpton Road bridge, taken in 1903, shows a group of Sunday afternoon strollers enjoying what was still a tranquil rural scene.

The date of this terrifyingly overloaded picnic excursion on the Lancaster Canal near Cadley is not known. However, the costumes suggest 1905 or thereabouts.

The canal remained in use for commercial traffic until the First World War, carrying lime from the Kendal and Carnforth area, coal brought from Glasson Dock (where it had been unloaded from coasters), slate from the Duddon, some agricultural produce and timber. The last mile into Preston was abandoned and largely filled in after the Second World War, but the remainder has survived and there are now serious plans to link the canal with the Ribble by a new waterway.

A wagon-and-four about to set out on an excursion from the Plough Tavern in Orchard Street to an unrecorded destination, 1907. If the men standing on the road were also going on the trip the wagon would be carrying no fewer than twenty-one people!

The old Preston railway station was described by Anthony Hewitson in 1882 as 'one of the most dismal, dilapidated, disgraceful-looking structures in Christendom . . . not only a very ill-looking, but an exceedingly inconvenient, dangerous station'. It was rebuilt in 1883, but this photograph (taken from the Fishergate bridge in 1862) shows the older building, a ramshackle collection of sheds and structures which, if the appalling state of the roof is any guide, certainly merited that derogatory description.

The Butler Street goods yard, 1862. On the left is the East Lancashire Railway engine shed, and on the right the ELR carriage shed and goods warehouse. In the centre is the London & North Western Railway's Charles Street goods depot. The site is now occupied by the Fishergate Centre and its car parks.

The North Union Railway bridge south of Preston station was built in 1836–8. It has been widened and altered on several occasions, but its scale and proportions are still impressive. In this photograph taken in 1862 the bridge of the East Lancashire Railway can be seen through the arch, with the large houses of Avenham at the top of the slope beyond.

The East Lancashire Railway from Todd Lane was opened in autumn 1850, and included a footbridge over the river, a favourite place for watching trains. Since it ran close to the exclusive houses of Avenham the bridges and embankments were landscaped. This photograph was taken in about 1900.

A third railway bridge across the Ribble was opened in 1882, when the West Lancashire Railway was extended from Longton to a new station at the foot of Fishergate Hill. The railway remained open for goods traffic until 1965, when the bridge was demolished except for an ugly iron pipe which now mars the setting of the old road bridge close by.

The branch line from Whittingham Asylum to the Longridge line at Grimsargh was operated from 1888 to 1957 and owned by the County Council. This photograph dates from about 1905. Although mainly for freight, the line did have a rudimentary passenger service on which hospital staff and visitors were carried free.

North of Preston station trains to Lancaster negotiated a sharp curve at Maudland, with a 10 m.p.h. speed limit. On the night of 13 July 1896 the Glasgow sleeper took the curve at an estimated 40 m.p.h. and was derailed. Only one person was killed, but the smash was spectacular; this view shows the tangled wreckage the next day. As a result of this accident the line was widened and the curve eased.

A horse-drawn tram on the Farringdon Park route at the cemetery gates, 1900. The horse-drawn trams of the Preston Tramways Company began operating to Fulwood in March 1879, and in 1882 the Corporation constructed additional routes to the cemetery and Farringdon Park, and to Ashton. These routes, with some later extensions, remained horse-drawn until 1903 when the Corporation converted them to electric traction.

The electric tram service began operation on 7 July 1904 at 7.10 a.m., when a car left the Lancaster Road for Fulwood via North Road. This postcard shows the first tram, watched by an early morning crowd. The Preston tramways were abandoned in favour of motorbuses in 1932–5.

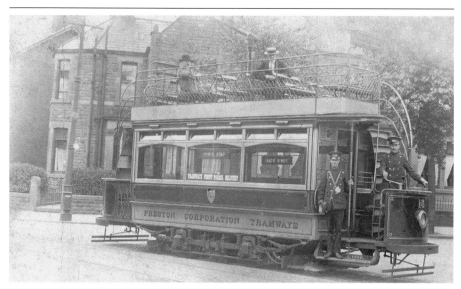

An electric tram on the Ashton route at Powis Road corner, *c.* 1910.

On Sundays there were short tram workings on the route to Farringdon Park, as far as the cemetery gates. The tram shown here (no. 10) has just arrived at the cemetery – the photograph is undated but was taken in about 1908.

Section Six

SCHOOLS AND CHURCHES

*The Home for the Blind for North and East Lancashire was opened in Lytham Road in
1895 and by 1902 housed forty children as well as adults. The foundation stone was laid
by the Countess of Derby, and she and Lord Derby opened it in 1895, so it was usually
called the Derby School for the Blind. It was closed, amid protests, in 1987.*

Pupils at the Royal Cross School for the Deaf, *c.* 1900. The school, at the top of Brockholes Brow, was endowed with the sum of £5,000 by Miss Cross of Red Scar and was opened by the Earl of Derby in 1894. Here children are being taught to lip-read using mirrors: confusing words with similar sounds are written out on the blackboard.

The exercise class at St Andrew's School, Ashton, *c*. 1905.

Serried ranks of schoolchildren and teachers staring intently at the camera were long a mainstay of photographers. This is St Mary's Street Wesleyan School Prize Choir in 1908. The headmaster, Mr Howarth, sits proudly in the centre; the pianist, Mr L. Margerison, is to his left. Samuel Woodruff is second on the left in the back row, and second on the right in the second row is Mattie Hampson.

The gymnasium group at the St Augustine's Roman Catholic Boys' School, precariously balanced in 1910.

The Preston Grammar School, on Cross Street, with Winckley Square and the Literary and Philosophical Institution in the background, *c.* 1900. The Grammar School was opened in 1841 and bought by the Corporation in 1860. In 1913 it moved to Moor Park Avenue, and the buildings were demolished in 1957.

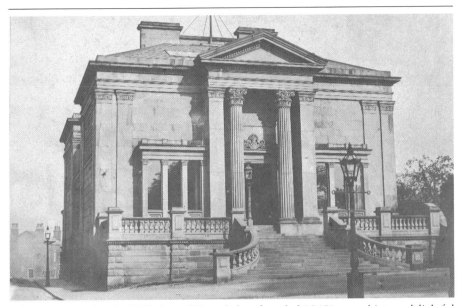

The Institution for the Diffusion of Knowledge (founded 1849) moved into a delightful Classical building at the end of Avenham Walk in 1850. The photograph was taken in 1863. In 1882 the Institution was endowed by the trustees of the late Edmund Harris and became a technical, scientific and art school, the Harris Institute. In 1932 it was converted into the Art College.

In 1895 work began on a new building for the Harris Institute, the Victoria Jubilee Technical School in Corporation Street (seen here in 1900). The Institute expanded continuously, and in 1956 became Harris College, which in 1970 was elevated into Preston (later Lancashire) Polytechnic. The culmination of its upward progress was its incorporation in 1992 as the University of Central Lancashire.

Edwin Beattie's small painting of the Roman Catholic chapel of St Mary in Friargate, sketched in about 1875. The church had a turbulent history. The first purpose-built Catholic chapel in the town was opened on this site in 1761, but it was destroyed by an anti-Catholic mob in 1768. Its replacement, built in 1770, was closed in 1793 when St Wilfrid's opened, as it was deemed superfluous to requirements. It became a cotton warehouse, but in 1815 it was restored and opened again for worship. It was pulled down in 1854 and replaced by the building painted by Beattie, but in 1991 this chapel was itself closed and demolished, amid great controversy.

The magnificent spire of the parish church dominates this view, taken from the roof of the Harris building early this century. The present church dates from 1854–5; its Gothic style has worn well and it is a crucial visual element in the town centre. Other churches visible include St James's, Avenham, and the unusual frontage of St Augustine's, with its two domed towers.

As Preston grew in the years after 1780 new suburbs began to develop, including Ashton on Ribble. By the 1830s this village had expanded sufficiently to justify the building of a new church. St Andrew's was opened in 1836, and is seen here, with the neighbouring vicarage, in 1863.

Christ Church, Fulwood (photographed 1863) was built in 1861 between Victoria Road and Higher Bank Road to serve the fashionable suburban development east of Garstang Road. Much of the area had been sold for building, as the Freehold Park Estate, in 1850. Exclusive low-density housing set in large gardens was developed along the attractive curving roads over the next twenty years.

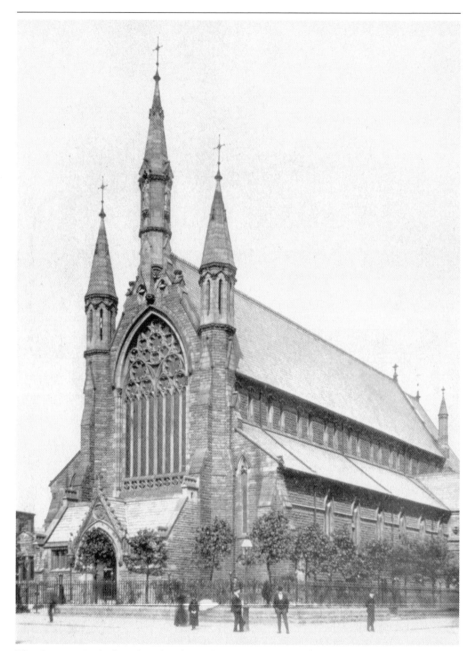

The Roman Catholic Church of St Thomas of Canterbury and the English Martyrs (usually known simply as 'English Martyrs') on Garstang Road was opened in 1867, after a long struggle to raise sufficient funds. The church was extended in 1888. The original designs were drawn up by Edward Welby Pugin, less famous son of A.W. Pugin, the great mid-Victorian architect.

Sharing with the Harris Museum the title of 'Preston's finest building', and the crowning glory of the town's very impressive skyline, is St Walburge's Church. The body of the church was built in 1848–54, and the marvellous 309 foot spire, the third highest in Britain, was added in 1856–66. It is seen here in the late 1890s as a church procession passes along Pedder Street.

The present frontage of St Augustine's Roman Catholic Church, one of the strangest buildings in Preston, was added in 1890 to the existing church which had been built in 1838–40. The photograph, taken in about 1888, shows the unaltered building, with its impressive Classical columns and portico.

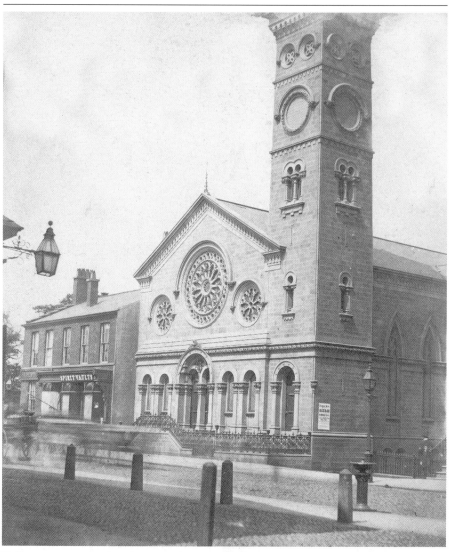

Fishergate Baptist Church, opened in 1858, was designed by a Preston man, James Hibbert, later the architect of the Harris Library and Museum. This photograph dates from 1862, and shows a blank clock-face: the clock was installed at the end of 1862. For a short period it was illuminated by gas at night, but complaints about the expense involved meant that this was abandoned in 1867, and the clock was not then lit until the 1882 Guild.

Section Seven

ENTERTAINMENTS AND THE ARTS

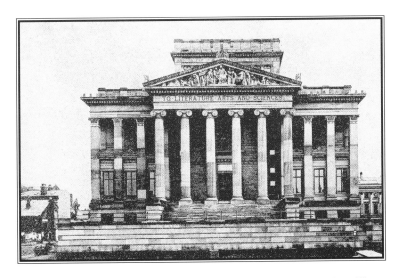

In the late nineteenth century the town centre was transformed by a series of major public

buildings which replaced the old properties around the market square. The most

outstanding was the Harris Library, one of the finest Greek Revival buildings in Britain.

Financed from the huge bequest made by Edmund Harris, it was opened in 1894.

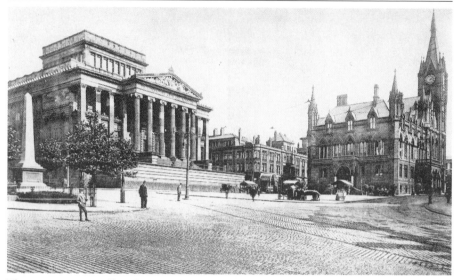

There was no overall architectural theme for the buildings of the market square – the result was a fascinating diversity of styles. In this 1912 photograph the Greek Revival Harris building and the High Victorian Gothic of the town hall are separated by the Edwardian American of the Miller Arcade. The visual loss resulting from the destruction of the town hall cannot be overstated.

In this curious photograph of the top of the Harris building, taken in about 1920, the antefixes around the pediment level, which are in the form of acanthus leaves, look like detached feet. In the distance are St Walburge's Church and north-west Preston.

The building was decorated with a profusion of classical images – casts of friezes and sculptures from antiquity and the Renaissance. The entrance hall was originally half-filled by this replica font and tabernacle (1430) from the Church of San Giovanni, Siena. Much of the superb decoration remains, beautifully restored in the 1980s; the building is of exceptional quality inside and outside.

The entrance hall and other circulating areas within the museum may have been lavishly decorated in keeping with the Victorian ideal of education by improving example, but the library lived up to another Victorian ideal – silent austerity. That is evident in this photograph of the Harris Library's reading room and newsroom, taken in 1903.

The cultural life of the Victorian town flourished, with many societies and clubs devoted to music, art, literature and science. Interest in technological and scientific progress prompted the establishment of the Preston Scientific Society: this is the Society's first photographic exhibition, held in its Cross Street rooms in 1897.

The Theatre Royal, Fishergate, painted in about 1830 by J. Ferguson. The theatre was built in 1802, and is architecturally no more than a plain box. It was altered in the 1840s, completely rebuilt in 1869, and likewise in 1882. Theatre Street is named after it.

Turn-of-the-century photographers often took photographs of children playing in and around the town. It does not do to be sentimental about these views – the children were usually desperately poor, and to see this as an 'age of innocence' would be wrong. Here a group of boys paddle in the Ribble beneath the old tram bridge in about 1910.

At the Whitsuntide holiday in 1896 a photographer recorded numerous scenes of entertainments in the centre of Preston. Here some boys set off to go fishing in the Ribble.

A small funfair was held on Whit Monday 1896 in the town centre, organized by Harrison's of Blackburn and Preston. This family firm operated swingboats, fairground amusements and hot pea saloons in many towns in mid-Lancashire during the late nineteenth and early twentieth centuries.

On the same day a boy had a small group of donkeys for hire in Market Street – a town version of the seaside donkey ride. Here they are seen waiting for the next customer.

The Whitsun Fairs remained a feature of Preston life until the Second World War. Here in the mid-1930s is Bert Hughes's fairground boxing booth, where 'professionals' waited to receive the challenges of allcomers. In the centre is Jack McCabe of Leyland.

Travelling curio shows were particularly popular in the years before the First World War. This postcard shows a bizarre exhibit from one such show – 'AFRIETA, THE MAN FISH', a grotesque parody of a mermaid. Made up of the lower half of a large fish and the upper part of a badly stuffed and moth-eaten monkey, it was displayed at the Queen's Hotel, Preston, in about 1900.

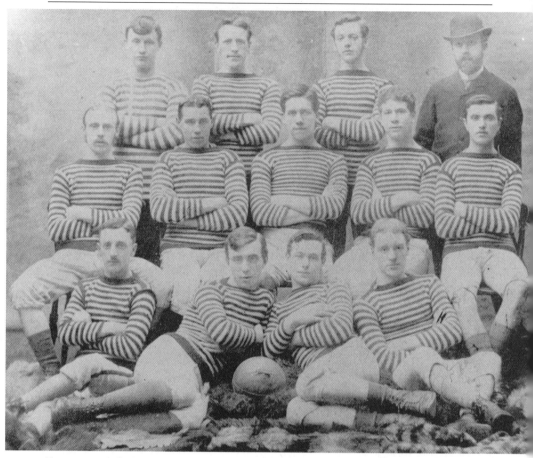

To many people Preston is synonymous with North End. The football team originated in 1878 when members of the Preston North End cricket team, which played on the edge of Moor Park at the north end of the town, began to play winter sports. By 1881, when this photograph was taken, North End had become one of the leading football teams in the north of England, attracting huge crowds to their Deepdale ground. The road to fame and glory had been taken.

On 1 May 1938 almost the entire town turned out to give the grandest of civic welcomes to Preston North End, who had just beaten Huddersfield Town 1–0 in the FA Cup Final at Wembley, before a crowd of 93,000 – their finest inter-war hour.

Although the Ribble was not officially navigable even as far as Penwortham old bridge, it was suitable for pleasure boating along the stretch from Penwortham past Miller and Avenham Parks. This photograph, taken in about 1890, shows a regatta, with the crews lining up outside the boat-house just below the North Union Railway viaduct.

The site of Avenham Park, seen from the garden of the Old Vicarage below Ribblesdale Place, 1863. The old tram bridge is prominent in the distance, and rising above the trees is the chimney of the steam engine which worked the incline. In the middle distance is Jackson's Farm. Landscaping of the park itself is in progress, but in contrast with today it is strikingly bare and treeless.

By 1900 the trees planted during the 1860s had matured sufficiently to give a well-wooded landscape. In this view, taken from the East Lancashire Railway bridge, the grand houses of Avenham and Ribblesdale Place can be seen at the top of the slope. In the foreground is the beautiful riverside avenue, still one of the finest features of the park.

With its extensive tree-planting and open grassland, Avenham Park quickly became a vital open space for the people of the densely packed housing areas of Avenham itself, Frenchwood and Larkhill areas. Here, in the early years of this century, are the steps at the Frenchwood end.

After its closure to freight traffic in the early 1860s the old tramway became a popular pedestrian path, and the bridge over the Ribble was a favoured place for Sunday walks. It made possible a circular route using both banks of the river, and gave access to the open countryside on the south side. It is shown here in about 1905.

The land which forms Miller Park was given to the town in 1864 by Alderman Thomas Miller. Its formal landscaping, with broad walks, fountains and statuary, contrasts with the informal and wooded appearance of Avenham Park. The two parks – physically divided by the East Lancashire Railway line – were a favourite place for holiday promenading. This photograph was taken on Easter Monday 1905.

On that day a large part of the town was out enjoying the sunshine, watching or participating in the egg-rolling ceremony, listening to the band or just walking around, seeing and being seen – as in this view of the great grassy bowl of Avenham Park.

Towering above Miller Park was the Park Hotel, a red-brick Victorian pile, full of style and panache but not especially successful as a hotel. Its setting was spoiled in the late 1960s when a concrete and glass tower block was built immediately alongside – ironically, this latter building houses the County Planning Department.

Moor Park is the finest open space north of the old town. Plum Pudding Hill (the origins of its name unknown) links Watling Street Road, via Lower Bank Road, with the park. When this photograph was taken in about 1906 the area was still important for horticulture and nursery-gardens, and on the left some of the glasshouses can be seen.

Moor Park was thronged on most public holidays. In contrast with Avenham and Miller Parks there was only limited formal landscaping, but instead there were longer walks and acres of grass. The mill chimneys of the town – on one of the few days each year when they were not belching out smoke – rise above the trees as hot-air balloons command excited attention, sometime around 1905.

Possibly on the same day, the swingboats and funfair are popular with the children.

MARKETS, SHOPS AND INNS

Preston's old market place was a fine sight in the early nineteenth century. The town still

had a wealth of half-timbered buildings, some of them of exceptional splendour – most of

these were demolished in the mid-1850s to make way for fashionable and up-to-date

Victorian stone and red-brick buildings, a great loss to the town's architectural heritage.

This imaginative painting by Paul Braddon shows the market place in about 1820, with

the Georgian town hall of 1762 in the background. In the centre is the obelisk, which was

erected for the Guild of 1782 and served – as this photograph suggests – as a market cross.

The Old Shambles in Lancaster Road, seen from Church Street, *c.* 1882. The photograph can be dated by the tramlines: the horse-drawn tramway from Lancaster Road to Fulwood was opened in 1879. The Shambles were built in 1715, and were intended primarily for use as butchers' stalls. These very interesting buildings were demolished in 1885 when the site was cleared to make way for the Harris Library and Museum.

In this extremely early photograph of the Market Square and Friargate the most prominent feature is the obelisk, which was demolished in 1853 and taken to Hollowforth (from which it returned in 1979). The photograph was therefore taken in about 1850–2. The buildings behind were cleared in 1893 to make way for Market Street and the new post office.

By the 1860s Preston urgently needed to replace the ramshackle stalls and shambles. Work on an iron-framed covered market hall started in 1869, but on 8 August 1870 the half-finished building collapsed. The area was said by the local paper to be 'strewn with a mass of detached and chaotic fragments – rent pillars, snapped girders, smashed tiles, severed ropes, broken poles – all heaped together in indescribable confusion'.

Earl Street and Market Street, *c.* 1906, showing the busy stalls selling second-hand shoes and clothes. The original covered market is on the right, but the later fishmarket has not yet been erected.

The Southport and Lytham shrimpers were a familiar sight in Preston market. This photograph, taken in about 1902, shows the Southport fishwives in their distinctive costume. As well as shellfish, many of them also sold inshore fish such as flounders, a speciality of the coast between the Ribble and the Mersey.

William Melling's stall at the fishmarket, August 1924. His family business dealt with fish and rabbits, and was based in Preston and Fleetwood.

Preston lay at the heart of Lancashire's cheese-making district, and its cheese market was by the late nineteenth century the largest in the county. The annual Cheese Fair, established in 1860, was of outstanding importance, and farmers and wholesalers from all over the region congregated in the town to inspect the vast array of cheeses exhibited. A magnificent display is seen here in the covered market during the 1906 show.

The Cheese Fair, 25 November 1913. Judging is apparently in progress. The decline of cheese-making in the inter-war period meant that the Preston fair did not survive, but north-west of the town is still one of the most important areas for 'authentic' farmhouse cheese production in England: proper Lancashire is a true delicacy and delight.

This celebrated late Victorian Preston character was an itinerant vendor of fly-papers. He always had a sticky fly-paper, well spotted with dead flies, wound round his hat, and he walked with a limp. Small boys would tease him 'until his indifference made his tormentors over-bold, and the stick would sweep forward with a deft twist of the wrist, and a howl of pain from some small boy'.

In 1889 Gregson's, the provision merchants of Hope Street, celebrated the 50th anniversary of their founding by Robert Gregson in 1839. They specialized in the curing of hams, a splendid collection of which can be seen hanging on the outside wall of the building, and were also the largest butter-dealers in North Lancashire.

The Preston Co-operative Society (founded 1873) was instrumental in improving the range and quality of foodstuffs available to the 'working classes'. The photograph shows the Marsh Lane store in about 1907, with a wide variety of fresh and tinned produce displayed in the windows. The shop was demolished in 1989 to make way for the Penwortham bypass extension.

Lipton's the grocers in Cheapside, *c*. 1895. The staff line up proudly for their photograph beneath a fine selection of rolls and joints of bacon and ham hanging up outside the shop – fewer environmental health rules then! Customers were left in no doubt that this was a quality shop, and that Lipton's was the royal grocer.

Racks of poultry and game, trays and marble slabs piled with fresh fish, and baskets and strings of fruit and vegetables – in 1902 Heaney's, the fruit and poultry merchant on the corner of Fishergate and Chapel Street was a feast for the eye. The proprietor, J.E. Gardner, can be seen bowler-hatted beneath the shop canopy.

The premises of J. Battersby, corn merchant, on the corner of Trafford Street and Wildman Street in Plungington, 1913. On the left can be seen the loading hoist, used to drop the laden sacks of corn into the waiting carts – a characteristic and easily recognizable feature of such buildings.

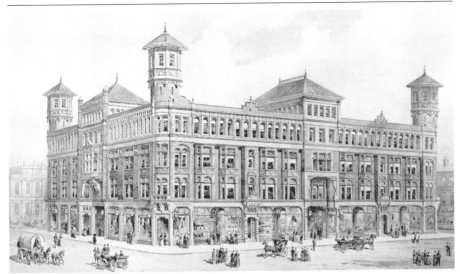

Miller Arcade (1901) had a new steel-framed construction technique derived from American skyscrapers. This architect's drawing emphasizes the very great care taken in the design of Preston's most fashionable and exclusive shopping development. Considerable artistic licence has been used: the town hall and the Harris building are omitted and it is in fact impossible to see the Miller Arcade from this perspective.

Preston's grandest hotel, now fallen on hard times, was the Bull and Royal. Formerly two inns, the White Bull and the Royal, it dates in part from the early seventeenth century, and has many historic associations. The Derby Room, with its beautiful plasterwork, was erected under the auspices of the twelfth Earl of Derby, who bought the hotel in 1773, as the setting for glittering social and political events.

The Virgins Inn, in Anchor Weind off Friargate, was the last thatched building in Preston; it probably dated from the sixeenth or early seventeenth century, and had it been spared it would now have been of immense historical interest. However, in 1894, just after this photograph was taken, it – together with a large area of adjacent property – was demolished to make way for the new post office building.

The Shoulder of Mutton Inn in the Old Shambles, Lancaster Road, was opposite the present Stanley Arms. It was pulled down, with the rest of the historic shambles, in 1882 to provide a site for the Harris Library, Museum and Art Gallery. This photograph was taken between 1879, when the tramway was laid, and 1882.

At the bottom of Fishergate Hill was the Regatta Inn, which originally catered for those pleasure-boating on the Ribble. Later the riverbank was built over by Allsupp's Shipyard, whose cranes can be seen in the background, and the boating ceased. The inn was demolished in June 1914 to make way for the new bridge to Penwortham – the site is now the road junction at the western end of the bridge.

The Grand Junction Hotel, at the busy junction of Watery Lane and Strand Road, was a favoured drinking place for dockers, and particularly important as the place where the foremen recruited casual labour. Here, in 1892, it is decorated with flags, and a small triumphal arch has been erected across Watery Lane, to welcome Prince Alfred, Duke of Edinburgh, who was officially to open the dock.

Section Nine

OUTER PRESTON

J. Jenkinson's famous picture of Preston from Penwortham Hill, painted in 1822 and copied in engravings and prints many times since, shows the old town in its beautiful rural setting, stretched along the low ridge above the river with the fells beyond. The industrialization of Preston was already well under way, as the smoking mill chimneys indicate, but the town was still small and it was only a short stroll into the fields in any direction.

This photograph, taken in Avenham Park in about 1904, is entitled 'The Three Grasshoppers'. It shows the cart on which grass clippings were collected. One of the boys, Harold Whitehead, later became Preston's Chief Fire Officer.

Two horses and a cart being used for the collecting of river pebbles (for cobbling streets and walls) below the tram bridge, *c.* 1900.

On the edge of Preston many farms remained well into this century, until the huge expansion of the built-up area, after 1920, led to the disappearance of many under a tide of bricks and mortar. Some of the farms specialized in dairying to supply the needs of the town. At the ancient farm of Higher Brockholes the dairy staff, with brightly polished churns, were photographed in 1911.

Also at Higher Brockholes, in 1911, the photographer took this superb photograph of the haymakers, a haunting image of a rural past which is now lost for ever.

The sixteenth-century house at Red Scar, overlooking the bend of the Ribble, was bought in the early nineteenth century by the Cross family, lawyers and politicians of Preston, and extended. It is seen here in about 1900. In 1929 Courtaulds purchased the estate and built a huge factory, but this was itself demolished in the early 1970s, to be replaced by the Red Scar industrial estate.

Cromwell Road, Ribbleton, 1906 (Langdale Road is on the left). In the late nineteenth century housing development began to extend eastwards from the town into areas of Ribbleton which had remained surprisingly rural. Rows of small semi-detached and terraced villas sprang up, but in 1906 Cromwell Road was still muddy and rutted, with the feel of a country lane.

The expansion of Preston in the inter-war period included the building by the Corporation of several large new housing estates to accommodate people displaced by slum clearance schemes in the town centre. This view shows Ribbleton Hall estate, built in the mid-1920s.

This detailed close-up of the old bridge at Penwortham, taken in 1863, shows us the chimneys of Preston beyond, and some houses appearing through the trees at the town end of Broadgate, but otherwise the bridge is still in a country setting. Forty years later, with trams at the opposite end of the bridge and new housing on both banks, much had changed.

Withy Trees Corner, Fulwood, *c.* 1920. Fulwood Wesleyan Methodist Church stands on the corner of Garstang Road and Watling Street Road. By this time Fulwood had become an important and high-class suburb of Preston, but it was not part of the borough – until 1974 it was administered by its own urban district council.

In Ashton on Ribble, in the mid-nineteenth century, a considerable area of small villas and attractive terraces in tree-lined roads was developed west of the Blackpool railway line. Wellington Road was one such street. It became the local shopping centre as this photograph, from about 1907, indicates.

As new suburbs appeared churches and chapels were established to serve the growing population of formerly rural areas. Here we see the ceremony in 1910 at which the foundation stone of the Fulwood Wesleyan Methodist Church was laid.

Section Ten

STREETS AND HOUSES

*Fishergate, 1882. In this view the architectural
diversity of the street is very apparent: a sequence
of different styles and periods, set off perfectly by
the soaring tower of the town hall, the overall
effect one of architectural quality and visual
interest. In contrast, the view today is largely
filled with bland and unimaginative shopfronts and
architecturally unremarkable post-war buildings.*

Until the 1940s the heart of Preston was around the upper end of Church Street, near the parish church. Seen here on 8 July 1913, decorated for the visit of George V and Queen Mary, are several imposing public buildings, including the Empire Theatre on the right. In the 1950s the area began to lose its status as the shopping centre shifted westwards, and today it is peripheral to the town centre.

Fishergate Hill, *c.* 1900. Originally a lane which led to the fisheries on the river, this became a fashionable residential area in the early nineteenth century. Large houses were built, but with the coming of the railway and the increase in traffic after the opening of the new bridge Fishergate Hill began to deteriorate. By the 1980s it was in a sorry state, with derelict properties and some of its best buildings demolished. Now there are hopeful signs of a long-overdue revival.

On 5 September 1903 a photographer standing at the top of St Mark's Church tower took this photograph to show, in the foreground, the crowds attending the ceremonial laying of the foundation stone of St Mark's parochial hall in Abbey Street. In the process he captured a memorable image of the combination of spires and chimneys which made up the Preston skyline.

Edwin Beattie's painting of the top end of Friargate, finished in 1893, shows the looming bulk of the new Harris building with market stalls in front. At the corner of the street is the group of sixteenth- and seventeenth-century buildings which were demolished in the following year to widen the entrance to Friargate – another work of improvement which in the process removed part of the old town and its architectural heritage.

The construction of Market Street and the building of the new block of shops and offices between the two roads widened the view down Friargate and reduced the enclosed feeling of the market place. Today, with the pedestrianization of Friargate, that feeling has to some extent been regained. This view was taken in about 1905.

Stoneygate, 1936. One of the oldest streets in Preston, this was the ancient route towards the bridge at Walton le Dale. In the last half-century almost all of its old property has been cleared and it now has open landscaping with grass and trees, but this was previously a narrow cobbled lane with many old (and by 1936 semi-derelict) buildings.

Arkwright House, Stoneygate, painted by J. Ferguson, *c.* 1850. The house was built for the master of the grammar school in the early eighteenth century. Richard Arkwright lodged there in 1768 and in his rooms worked secretly on perfecting the mechanism of his water frame. David Hunt, in his *History of Preston*, says that this building 'may justly claim to have been one of the birthplaces of the Industrial Revolution'.

Anchor Court, looking towards the market square, *c.* 1912. This narrow winding street, typical of the old town, was part of a convoluted network of such lanes behind Friargate. It is now, sad to say, the ugly service road behind the St George's Centre.

Lowthian Street was once Plant's Court, a very narrow passage which ran from the Hippodrome in Friargate through to Starch House Square. The street has kept much of its gloomy enclosed atmosphere, and is one of the few parts of the town centre where the character of the mid-nineteenth century is still apparent.

Back Lane, 1879. This cobbled lane ran behind Friargate, and this view was taken from what is now the junction of Market Street and Earl Street, looking towards the market square. All these buildings were demolished in 1895 to allow construction of Market Street, which roughly follows the line of the lane shown.

Everton Gardens from Fell Street in about 1935, before the area was razed for slum clearance. The site is now occupied by the bus station. Everton Gardens was a particularly narrow lane of tiny cottages, built in the late eighteenth century – 'gardens' seems a most incongruous name for such a place, which had some of the worst housing in late nineteenth-century Preston.

Terraced houses built in the mid-1790s for handloom weavers, in Mount Pleasant Street West (off Corporation Street), *c.* 1930. They were demolished in September 1952 and the site is now the car park behind the County Library Headquarters, whose building in Bowran Street can be seen in the background.

Early industrial housing in Hardman's Yard, Friargate, pulled down in 1926. This scene, with small cottages crammed into the narrow plots which lay behind the street frontage of Friargate, was typical of the first phase of the Preston's industrial growth, during the years from 1790 to 1830. In 1862 this yard contained twenty-one houses, in which ninety-three people lived and shared just three privies. With minor exceptions the hundreds of cottages built near the town centre during this period have been demolished, but enough were photographed in the 1920s and '30s to give at least a partial impression of their character and their terrible squalor.

In stark contrast with the previous view, but only 400 yards away, is the east side of Winckley Square, 1862. The square was laid out as an exclusive residential area at the very beginning of the ninteenth century. There was no overall building scheme, and no attempt to produce a grand formal design, and the result was a pleasing diversity of buildings and styles. Individual property owners employed their own architects and displayed their own aesthetic tastes, and this gave a very effective 'unity in diversity', as this view illustrates.

The Italianate villa at the corner of Winckley Square and Cross Street, home of the cotton manufacturer William Ainsworth, 1862. Like many other properties on this side of the square it was demolished in the 1960s, a time when immense damage was done to Preston's rich architectural heritage.

Winckley Square was the most exclusive residential area in early nineteenth-century Preston, and remained so until the 1860s and '70s, when its proximity to the noisy and busy town centre meant that it had less appeal to wealthy residents, who then began to move out to the suburbs. This view shows the south side of the square in 1862, with the original entrance gates which provided additional privacy to the occupants of the grand houses.

The west end of Avenham Lane, showing the entrance to Avenham Terrace, 1862. Avenham House is in the centre, behind the trees. The sleepy, tranquil atmosphere which this corner of Preston enjoyed in the mid-nineteenth century is very clear from this and the previous view. The growth of motor traffic in the early twentieth century helped to destroy the peace, and the busy traffic on Avenham Lane is now a major problem.

Acknowledgements

All the photographs in this book are taken from the collections of the Harris Museum and Art Gallery, Preston, and the first acknowledgement must be to the museum staff and in particular to Sally Coleman, Senior Keeper of Social History, who has given invaluable help and assistance in the preparation of the book. It is especially important that material such as this is made accessible to a wider readership, and this book represents an important means of achieving that end. I am very grateful to Preston Borough Council for giving its support to the project and for allowing photographs in its possession to be reproduced.

Special thanks and acknowledgement are also due to all those people of Preston and elsewhere who have, over the past century, donated photographs to the museum. Without their generosity it would have been quite impossible to compile this photographic record, and I hope that this will encourage others to follow suit and consider gifts of this sort in the future.

The fruits of some of my own researches on the history of the town have been published elsewhere, but I would like to acknowledge the work of Preston's other historians, past and present. In particular I should mention, among those long gone, Richard Kuerden, Anthony Hewitson and William Clemesha, and among those who are happily still flourishing it is a pleasure to thank David Hunt, Stephen Sartin, Nigel Morgan, Marian Roberts and Geoff Timmins.

BRITAIN IN OLD PHOTOGRAPHS

To order any of these titles please telephone Littlehampton Book Services on 01903 721596

ALDERNEY

Alderney: A Second Selection, *B Bonnard*

BEDFORDSHIRE

Bedfordshire at Work, *N Lutt*

BERKSHIRE

Maidenhead, *M Hayles & D Hedges*
Around Maidenhead, *M Hayles & B Hedges*
Reading, *P Southerton*
Reading: A Second Selection, *P Southerton*
Sandhurst and Crowthorne, *K Dancy*
Around Slough, *J Hunter & K Hunter*
Around Thatcham, *P Allen*
Around Windsor, *B Hedges*

BUCKINGHAMSHIRE

Buckingham and District, *R Cook*
High Wycombe, *R Goodearl*
Around Stony Stratford, *A Lambert*

CHESHIRE

Cheshire Railways, *M Hitches*
Chester, *S Nichols*

CLWYD

Clwyd Railways, *M Hitches*

CLYDESDALE

Clydesdale, *Lesmahagow Parish Historical Association*

CORNWALL

Cornish Coast, *T Bowden*
Falmouth, *P Gilson*
Lower Fal, *P Gilson*
Around Padstow, *M McCarthy*
Around Penzance, *J Holmes*
Penzance and Newlyn, *J Holmes*
Around Truro, *A Lyne*
Upper Fal, *P Gilson*

CUMBERLAND

Cockermouth and District, *J Bernard Bradbury*
Keswick and the Central Lakes, *J Marsh*
Around Penrith, *F Boyd*
Around Whitehaven, *H Fancy*

DERBYSHIRE

Derby, *D Buxton*
Around Matlock, *D Barton*

DEVON

Colyton and Seaton, *T Gosling*
Dawlish and Teignmouth, *G Gosling*
Devon Aerodromes, *K Saunders*
Exeter, *P Thomas*
Exmouth and Budleigh Salterton, *T Gosling*
From Haldon to Mid-Dartmoor, *T Hall*
Honiton and the Otter Valley, *J Yallop*
Around Kingsbridge, *K Tanner*
Around Seaton and Sidmouth, *T Gosling*
Seaton, Axminster and Lyme Regis, *T Gosling*

DORSET

Around Blandford Forum, *B Cox*
Bournemouth, *M Colman*
Bridport and the Bride Valley, *J Burrell & S Humphries*
Dorchester, *T Gosling*
Around Gillingham, *P Crocker*

DURHAM

Darlington, *G Flynn*
Darlington: A Second Selection, *G Flynn*
Durham People, *M Richardson*
Houghton-le-Spring and Hetton-le-Hole, *K Richardson*
Houghton-le-Spring and Hetton-le-Hole:
  A Second Selection, *K Richardson*
Sunderland, *S Miller & B Bell*
Teesdale, *D Coggins*
Teesdale: A Second Selection, *P Raine*
Weardale, *J Crosby*
Weardale: A Second Selection, *J Crosby*

DYFED

Aberystwyth and North Ceredigion,
  Dyfed Cultural Services Dept
Haverfordwest, *Dyfed Cultural Services Dept*
Upper Tywi Valley, *Dyfed Cultural Services Dept*

ESSEX

Around Grays, *B Evans*

GLOUCESTERSHIRE

Along the Avon from Stratford to Tewkesbury, *J Jeremiah*
Cheltenham: A Second Selection, *R Whiting*
Cheltenham at War, *P Gill*
Cirencester, *J Welsford*
Around Cirencester, *E Cuss & P Griffiths*
Forest, The, *D Mullin*
Gloucester, *J Voyce*
Around Gloucester, *A Sutton*
Gloucester: From the Walwin Collection, *J Voyce*
North Cotswolds, *D Viner*
Severn Vale, *A Sutton*
Stonehouse to Painswick, *A Sutton*
Stroud and the Five Valleys, *S Gardiner & L Padin*
Stroud and the Five Valleys: A Second Selection,
  S Gardiner & L Padin
Stroud's Golden Valley, *S Gardiner & L Padin*
Stroudwater and Thames & Severn Canals,
  E Cuss & S Gardiner
Stroudwater and Thames & Severn Canals: A Second
  Selection, *E Cuss & S Gardiner*
Tewkesbury and the Vale of Gloucester, *C Hilton*
Thornbury to Berkeley, *J Hudson*
Uley, Dursley and Cam, *A Sutton*
Wotton-under-Edge to Chipping Sodbury, *A Sutton*

GWYNEDD

Anglesey, *M Hitches*
Gwynedd Railways, *M Hitches*
Around Llandudno, *M Hitches*
Vale of Conwy, *M Hitches*

HAMPSHIRE

Gosport, *J Sadden*
Portsmouth, *P Rogers & D Francis*

HEREFORDSHIRE

Herefordshire, *A Sandford*

HERTFORDSHIRE

Barnet, *I Norrie*
Hitchin, *A Fleck*
St Albans, *S Mullins*
Stevenage, *M Appleton*

ISLE OF MAN

The Tourist Trophy, *B Snelling*

ISLE OF WIGHT

Newport, *D Parr*
Around Ryde, *D Parr*

JERSEY

Jersey: A Third Selection, *R Lemprière*

KENT

Bexley, *M Scott*
Broadstairs and St Peter's, *J Whyman*
Bromley, Keston and Hayes, *M Scott*
Canterbury: A Second Selection, *D Butler*
Chatham and Gillingham, *P MacDougall*
Chatham Dockyard, *P MacDougall*
Deal, *J Broady*
Early Broadstairs and St Peter's, *B Wootton*
East Kent at War, *D Collyer*
Eltham, *J Kennett*
Folkestone: A Second Selection, *A Taylor & E Rooney*
Goudhurst to Tenterden, *A Guilmant*
Gravesend, *R Hiscock*
Around Gravesham, *R Hiscock & D Grierson*
Herne Bay, *J Hawkins*
Lympne Airport, *D Collyer*
Maidstone, *I Hales*
Margate, *R Clements*
RAF Hawkinge, *R Humphreys*
RAF Manston, *RAF Manston History Club*
RAF Manston: A Second Selection,
  RAF Manston History Club
Ramsgate and Thanet Life, *D Perkins*
Romney Marsh, *E Carpenter*
Sandwich, *C Wanostrocht*
Around Tonbridge, *C Bell*
Tunbridge Wells, *M Rowlands & I Beavis*
Tunbridge Wells: A Second Selection,
  M Rowlands & I Beavis
Around Whitstable, *C Court*
Wingham, Adisham and Littlebourne, *M Crane*

LANCASHIRE

Around Barrow-in-Furness, *J Garbutt & J Marsh*
Blackpool, *C Rothwell*
Bury, *J Hudson*
Chorley and District, *J Smith*
Fleetwood, *C Rothwell*
Heywood, *J Hudson*
Around Kirkham, *C Rothwell*
Lancashire North of the Sands, *J Garbutt & J Marsh*
Around Lancaster, *S Ashworth*
Lytham St Anne's, *C Rothwell*
North Fylde, *C Rothwell*
Radcliffe, *J Hudson*
Rossendale, *B Moore & N Dunnachie*

LEICESTERSHIRE

Around Ashby-de-la-Zouch, *K Hillier*
Charnwood Forest, *I Keil, W Humphrey & D Wix*
Leicester, *D Burton*
Leicester: A Second Selection, *D Burton*
Melton Mowbray, *T Hickman*
Around Melton Mowbray, *T Hickman*
River Soar, *D Wix, P Shacklock & I Keil*
Rutland, *T Clough*
Vale of Belvoir, *T Hickman*
Around the Welland Valley, *S Mastoris*

LINCOLNSHIRE

Grimsby, *J Tierney*
Around Grimsby, *J Tierney*
Grimsby Docks, *J Tierney*
Lincoln, *D Cuppleditch*